Paean to Apollo:
A 21st Century Hymn

Peter L. Smith

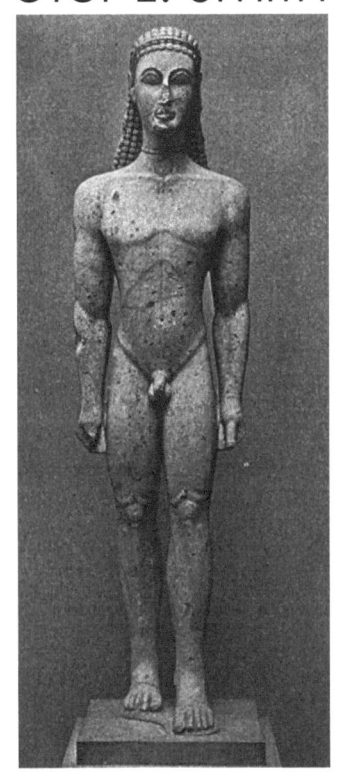

Paean to Apollo: A 21st Century Hymn

Paean to Apollo: A 21st Century Hymn (Copyright © 2010) by Peter L. Smith. All rights reserved. Printed in the United States of America. No part of this book may be used or reproduced in any manner whatsoever without written permission except in the case of brief quotations embodied in critical articles and reviews. For information, address TARANIS BOOKS, 1009 Cumberland Avenue, San Leandro, CA 94579. FIRST EDITION Cover and layout designed by Peter L. Smith.

ISBN: 978-0-557-39965-9

Paean to Apollo
A 21st Century Hymn

Peter L. Smith

Paean to Apollo: A 21st Century Hymn

πετερ
ληνν
σμιθ

ωπη'

DCCCLXXXVII

Paean to Apollo: A 21st Century Hymn

*Since to thy care,
the figur'd seal's consign'd,*

*Which stamps
the world with forms
of ev'ry kind.*

*Hear me, blest pow'r,
and in these rites rejoice,*

*And save thy mystics with a
suppliant voice.*

Paean to Apollo: A 21st Century Hymn

Acknowledgements

Any observant reader will readily understand that whatever creative element exists in this work consists in the tailoring and emphasis and re-arranging of those parts of the ancient hymns to Apollo that may strike home closest to the ear of the early 21st century seeker. Of course, the photos are taken from royalty free sources and so are unattributed.
I hasten to add that the following mantra:

PYTHION APOLLON APOLLON PYTHION PAIAN

was created at my request by Todd Jackson. My thanks to this tireless scholar and advocate of the worship of Apollo across the world. You may find more about modern-day worship of Apollo at:

http://www.facebook.com/group.php?gid=79552461480

Paean to Apollo: A 21st Century Hymn

Paean to Apollo: A 21st Century Hymn

Φ

A book to assist
in litany
to the most ancient of gods

the one to whom all
olympianS Tremble and bow

and to whom now,
perhaps, billions, pray
but veil'd;

veil'd i say.

may thy veil be removed!
and by thy propitious name
may all come to light!
and your chosen
thy sweetness

. . . know.

Paean to Apollo: A 21st Century Hymn

The Orphic Hymn to Apollo

Blest Paean, come, propitious to my pray'r,
Illustrious pow'r, whom Memphian tribes revere,
Slayer of Tityus, and the God of health,
Lycorian Phoebus, fruitful source of wealth.

Spermatic, golden-lyr'd, the field from thee
Receives it's constant, rich fertility.

Titanic, Grunian, Smynthian, thee I sing,
Python-destroying, hallow'd, Delphian king:
Rural, light-bearer, and the Muse's head,
Noble and lovely, arm'd with arrows dread:
Far-darting, Bacchian, two-fold, and divine,
Pow'r far diffused, and course oblique is thine.

O, Delian king, whose light-producing eye
Views all within, and all beneath the sky:
Whose locks are gold, whose oracles are sure,
Who, omens good reveal'st, and precepts pure:

Hear me entreating for the human kind,
Hear, and be present with benignant mind;
For thou survey'st this boundless aether all,
And ev'ry part of this terrestrial ball
Abundant, blessed; and thy piercing sight,
Extends beneath the gloomy, silent night;
Beyond the darkness, starry-ey'd, profound,
The stable roots, deep fix'd by thee are found.

Paean to Apollo: A 21st Century Hymn

The world's wide bounds, all-flourishing are thine,
Thyself all the source and end divine:
'Tis thine all Nature's music to inspire,
With various-sounding, harmonising lyre;
Now the last string thou tun'ft to sweet accord,
Divinely warbling now the highest chord;
Th' immortal golden lyre, now touch'd by thee,
Responsive yields a Dorian melody.

All Nature's tribes to thee their diff'rence owe,
And changing seasons from thy music flow
Hence, mix'd by thee in equal parts, advance
Summer and Winter in alternate dance;
This claims the highest, that the lowest string,
The Dorian measure tunes the lovely spring.

Hence by mankind, Pan-royal, two-horn'd nam'd,
Emitting whistling winds thro' Syrinx fam'd;
Since to thy care, the figur'd seal's consign'd,
Which stamps the world with forms of ev'ry kind.

Hear me, blest pow'r, and in these rites rejoice,
And save thy mystics
with a suppliant voice.

Translation by Thomas Taylor

Paean to Apollo: A 21st Century Hymn

May this be a guide to worship and contemplation.

This can be read at any time, but most efficaciously read at the precise moment that the sun rises on the temple of Apollo at Delphi.

38°29'N 22°30'E; GMT +2

Paean to Apollo: A 21st Century Hymn

Paean to Apollo:

A 21st Century Hymn

Peter L. Smith

Paean to Apollo: A 21st Century Hymn

The First Septenary:

THE GLORIOUS MYSTERIES

Paean to Apollo: A 21st Century Hymn

a'
one

O blessed one, hear the suppliant voice of the initiates and save them.

PAIAN PYTHION APOLLON
APOLLON PYTHION PAIAN

Paean to Apollo: A 21st Century Hymn

β'
two

O glorious youth.

PAIAN PYTHION APOLLON
APOLLON PYTHION PAIAN

Paean to Apollo: A 21st Century Hymn

Υ'
three

You are a wild, light-bringing and lovable God.

PAIAN PYTHION APOLLON
APOLLON PYTHION PAIAN

Paean to Apollo: A 21st Century Hymn

δ'

four

Always fair, always young

PAIAN PYTHION APOLLON
APOLLON PYTHION PAIAN

Paean to Apollo: A 21st Century Hymn

ε'
five

Never do Traces of down touch his blooming cheeks.

PAIAN PYTHION APOLLON
APOLLON PYTHION PAIAN

Paean to Apollo: A 21st Century Hymn

στ'
six

His hair drips fragrant oils to the ground,

PAIAN PYTHION APOLLON
APOLLON PYTHION PAIAN

Paean to Apollo: A 21st Century Hymn

ζ'
seven

> # You shoot your arrows from afar.

PAIAN PYTHION APOLLON
APOLLON PYTHION PAIAN

Apollo

Paean to Apollo: A 21st Century Hymn

Paean to Apollo: A 21st Century Hymn

The Second Septenary:
THE MAJESTIC MYSTERIES

Paean to Apollo: A 21st Century Hymn

η'
eight

Golden is your hair, and clear your oracular utterance.

*PAIAN PYTHION APOLLON
APOLLON PYTHION PAIAN*

Paean to Apollo: A 21st Century Hymn

θ'
nine

You lead the Muses into dance.

PAIAN PYTHION APOLLON
APOLLON PYTHION PAIAN

Paean to Apollo: A 21st Century Hymn

I'

ten

> You see earth's roots below, and you hold the bounds of the whole world.

PAIAN PYTHION APOLLON
APOLLON PYTHION PAIAN

Paean to Apollo: A 21st Century Hymn

ια'
eleven

You have the master seal of the entire cosmos.

PAIAN PYTHION APOLLON
APOLLON PYTHION PAIAN

Paean to Apollo: A 21st Century Hymn

ιβ'
twelve

As he goes through the house of Zeus, the gods tremble before him

PAIAN PYTHION APOLLON
APOLLON PYTHION PAIAN

Paean to Apollo: A 21st Century Hymn

ΙΓ'
thirteen

All spring up from their seats when he draws near, as he bends his bright bow.

PAIAN PYTHION APOLLON
APOLLON PYTHION PAIAN

Paean to Apollo: A 21st Century Hymn

ιδ'
fourteen

> I will remember and not be unmindful of Apollo who shoots afar.

PAIAN PYTHION APOLLON
APOLLON PYTHION PAIAN

Apollo (1898 Drawing)

Paean to Apollo: A 21st Century Hymn

The Third Septenary:
THE MYSTIC MYSTERIES

Paean to Apollo: A 21st Century Hymn

ιε'
fifteen

How, then, shall I sing of you who in all ways are a worthy theme of song?

PAIAN PYTHION APOLLON
APOLLON PYTHION PAIAN

Paean to Apollo: A 21st Century Hymn

Ιστ΄
sixteen

In this place I am minded to build a glorious temple to be an oracle for men.

*PAIAN PYTHION APOLLON
APOLLON PYTHION PAIAN*

Paean to Apollo: A 21st Century Hymn

ιζ'
seventeen

Here they will always bring perfect hecatombs.

PAIAN PYTHION APOLLON
APOLLON PYTHION PAIAN

Paean to Apollo: A 21st Century Hymn

ιη'
eighteen

They who dwell in rich Peloponnesus and [in] Europe and all the wave-washed isles, [shall come] to question me.

PAIAN PYTHION APOLLON
APOLLON PYTHION PAIAN

Paean to Apollo: A 21st Century Hymn

ιθ'
nineteen

And I will deliver to them all counsel that cannot fail, answering them in my rich temple.

PAIAN PYTHION APOLLON
APOLLON PYTHION PAIAN

Paean to Apollo: A 21st Century Hymn

κ'

twenty

Lord, since you have brought us here far from our dear ones and our fatherland, tell us now how we shall live.

PAIAN PYTHION APOLLON
APOLLON PYTHION PAIAN

Paean to Apollo: A 21st Century Hymn

κα'
twenty-one

We would know of you

PAIAN PYTHION APOLLON
APOLLON PYTHION PAIAN

Paean to Apollo: A 21st Century Hymn

The Fourth Septenary:
THE PRIESTLY MYSTERIES

Paean to Apollo: A 21st Century Hymn

κβ'

twenty-two

This land is not to be desired either for vineyards or for pastures so that we can live well thereon and also minister to men.

PAIAN PYTHION APOLLON
APOLLON PYTHION PAIAN

Paean to Apollo: A 21st Century Hymn

κγ'
twenty-three

> Foolish mortals and poor drudges are you, that you seek cares and hard toils and straits!

PAIAN PYTHION APOLLON
APOLLON PYTHION PAIAN

Paean to Apollo: A 21st Century Hymn

κδ'
twenty-four

Easily will I tell you a word and set it in your hearts.

PAIAN PYTHION APOLLON
APOLLON PYTHION PAIAN

Paean to Apollo: A 21st Century Hymn

κε'
twenty-five

> Though each one of you with knife in hand should slaughter sheep continually, yet would you always have abundant store, even all that the glorious tribes of men bring here for me.

PAIAN PYTHION APOLLON
APOLLON PYTHION PAIAN

Paean to Apollo: A 21st Century Hymn

κστ'
twenty-six

But guard you my temple and receive the tribes of men that gather to this place.

PAIAN PYTHION APOLLON
APOLLON PYTHION PAIAN

Paean to Apollo: A 21st Century Hymn

κζ'
twenty-seven

And especially show mortal men my will, and do you keep righteousness in your heart.

PAIAN PYTHION APOLLON
APOLLON PYTHION PAIAN

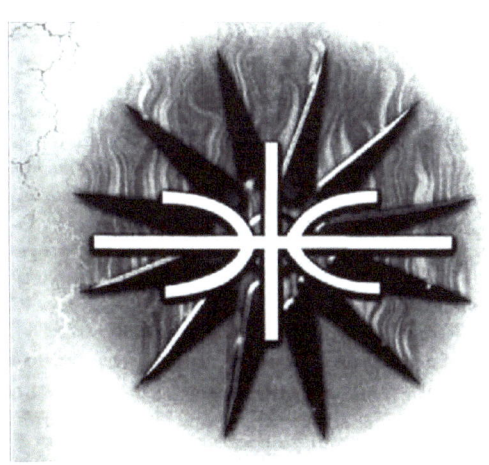

Paean to Apollo: A 21st Century Hymn

κη'
twenty-eight

[Let none be] disobedient [or] pay no heed to my warning.

PAIAN PYTHION APOLLON
APOLLON PYTHION PAIAN

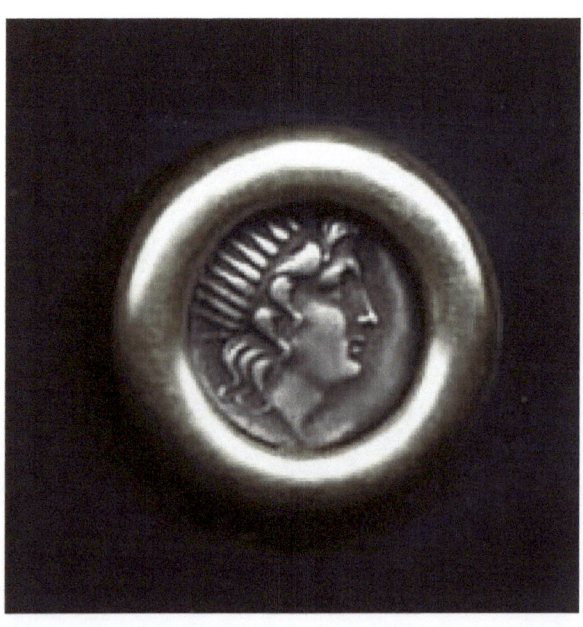

Paean to Apollo: A 21st Century Hymn

The Fifth Septenary:

THE HOLY MYSTERIES

Paean to Apollo: A 21st Century Hymn

κθ'

twenty-nine

[Let there be no] idle word or deed [or] outrage as is common among mortal men.

PAIAN PYTHION APOLLON
APOLLON PYTHION PAIAN

Paean to Apollo: A 21st Century Hymn

λ'

thirty

> [Or else] other men shall be your masters and with a strong hand shall make you subject for ever

*PAIAN PYTHION APOLLON
APOLLON PYTHION PAIAN*

Apollo. Roman statue by Apollonius. Photo ©Mercur Förlag-GML

Paean to Apollo: A 21st Century Hymn

λα'

thirty-one

Apollon Aristaisos [*best*]; Apollon Boedromios [*rescuer*]; Apollon Epikourios [*ally*]

PAIAN PYTHION APOLLON
APOLLON PYTHION PAIAN

Paean to Apollo: A 21st Century Hymn
λβ'
thirty-two

Apollon Hersos *[divine child]*;
Apollon Iatros *[doctor]*;
Apollon Kourotrophos
[protector of youth].

PAIAN PYTHION APOLLON
APOLLON PYTHION PAIAN

Paean to Apollo: A 21st Century Hymn

λγ'

thirty-three

Apollon Luekatas
[of the light];
Apollon Nomios [Shepherd];
Apollon Parnopios
[of the Plague of Locusts].

PAIAN PYTHION APOLLON
APOLLON PYTHION PAIAN

Paean to Apollo: A 21st Century Hymn
λδ'
thirty-four

Apollon Phoibos
[bright];
Apollon Proospsios
[foreseeing];
Apollon Spodios
[of the ashes]

PAIAN PYTHION APOLLON
APOLLON PYTHION PAIAN

Paean to Apollo: A 21st Century Hymn

λε'

thirty-five

Apollon Thearios

[oracular];

Apollon Theoxenios

[God of Strangers]

PAIAN PYTHION APOLLON
APOLLON PYTHION PAIAN

Paean to Apollo: A 21st Century Hymn

PAIAN PYTHION APOLLON!
APOLLON PYTHION PAIAN!

PAIAN PYTHION APOLLON!
APOLLON PYTHION PAIAN!

PAIAN PYTHION APOLLON
APOLLON PYTHION PAIAN!

www.ingramcontent.com/pod-product-compliance
Lightning Source LLC
Chambersburg PA
CBHW040016240426
43664CB00036B/11